THE SCARLET FOUNDRY TAROT ALMANAC 2014

WRITTEN BY
CHRISTINA LARSON

COVER IMAGE BY
AN-MAGI ERLANDSEN

PUBLISHED BY
Lulu Enterprises
2013

ISBN 978-1-304-34570-7

Table of Contents

Hello!

Welcome to 2014! It is going to be an interesting year. Hopefully this little book will help you navigate the cosmic terrain! I have provided love, career and general readings for every sign of the Zodiac. There is also a month by month psychic-weather forecast for each of you.

Please visit my website for more information or to make an appointment for a reading!

www.scarletfoundry.com

Enjoy,

Xtina

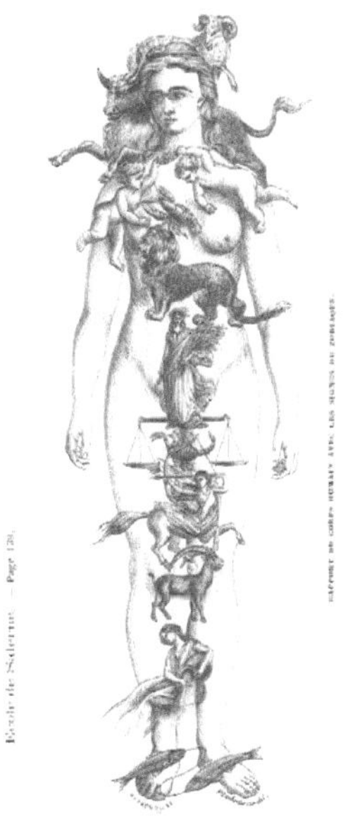

The beautiful cover image is by An-Magi of Tarot of the Pomegranate. She is painting her own tarot deck. Check it out at www.tarotofthepomegranate.com.

2014 GENERAL FORECAST

2014 will be rolling in with a powerful and exciting energy. It is asking all of us to balance our desire for short term gratification with the deeper experience of accomplishing a long term goal. Luckily, it will be easier than usual to have excellent follow through and accomplish tasks that improve quality of life. If there something that you have attempted to do in the past, maybe several times, that you haven't quite been able to achieve, this is the year to finally *do it!*

The motto for 2014 is 'failure is only temporary'. At some point in our lives it is also inevitable. What is your relationship to failure? Do you let it destroy you and your motivation? It takes courage to use failure as a learning tool and keep moving forward. Persevering through challenges shows yourself and others how badly you want something and also makes a hard won achievement sweeter!

Disciplined effort now leads to freedom later. Harnessing and focusing your energies is necessary to success and a sense of personal integrity. Pay attention to where you spend your money, what you put in your mouth and how you treat others. Every decision, everyday, creates your reality now and the life you will live in the future. Everything builds upon itself and everything matters. If you want to change your future, change your habits today.

This year is *the* year to take total responsibility for your happiness and release any blame for an unsatisfying life on others. Be creative, excited and ambitious! You are the captain of your ship, and it is up to you to get yourself to your destination. Bon Voyage!

The Chariot

♋♌♍♎♏♐♑♒♓

Here are the universal energy patterns that will govern each month in 2014. Every season has its own messages. Read the personal monthly meditation for your sign and put it in this seasonal context!

WINTER TRILOGY

JANUARY:

If you want extraordinary results, you need to take extraordinary measures. Don't keep doing the same thing if you want a different outcome. Life responds to your energy, so step it up to the next level and see what you are capable of.

FEBRUARY:

Join a group or organization to feel part of a greater whole. Don't ignore spiritual restlessness, explore it. If everyday life is feeling like a grind, it is because you need more connection and mystery in your reality.

MARCH:

A joyful, warm energy enters the scene. New relationships may bloom like the first flowers popping up from the cold spring ground. A sense of safety comes with clarity about a situation.

.*SPRING TRILOGY*

APRIL:

It is a good month to spend quality time alone, making your master plan to rule the world. Don't worry about missing the party! There will always be more parties. Right now you need to make a map of where you are going. Distracting yourself is a big waste of time.

MAY:

Taking a risk for happiness will pay off magnificently. The unknown is where luck lays so jump into a new situation or opportunity with excitement and trust. Release your need to control the outcome.

JUNE:

Action is where the action is! You are capable of achieving anything you put your mind to, so just do it. It is time to launch an idea or concept into the world. Take practical steps to create a magical reality.

SUMMER TRILOGY

JULY:

If you are single you may start a significant love relationship this summer. If you are in a relationship it may deepen and go to the next level of commitment. Are you ready? It is a good time to analyze your relationship to commitment and figure out where it fits in to your life.

AUGUST:

Your life is a piece of art. You came out of nothing and now you exist; the ultimate creative act. Keep the momentum by adding new elements and embellishments to your life. Persevere to create the most beautiful masterpiece you are capable of.

SEPTEMBER:

You are never trapped. You always have freedom of choice. If you feel caught in a situation or habit, realize you have the power to free yourself. Your subconscious self is powerful now…for better or worse. Creativity and passion live there, but so do jealousy and darker things. Try to be accepting of your imperfections.

AUTUMN TRILOGY

OCTOBER:

You don't have all the information! Hold off on reacting or deciding a little longer. Either you need to do more research about a pending situation, or get the full truth out of someone who has been less than forthcoming. Dreams are powerful now.

NOVEMBER:

Freewill and luck intersect in an unforgettable way. Any effort put forth will be rewarded by a surprising turn of events. Expect the unexpected! In time you will understand exactly why everything happened the way it did.

DECEMBER: It is just about time for the fairytale to end with 'happily ever after'. The dragon has been slayed, the lessons learned. It is time to reap the rewards of your effort and rest up before the new story begins.

---*All life is an experiment. Make as many experiments as possible.*

Ralph Waldo Emerson

ARIES

Overview

In 2014 Aries will be able to capitalize on the skills they have acquired over the past few years. Don't be afraid to launch your own business or put your dream into action. Some of you have been learning a new trade or craft and now is the time to bring it into the real world. Go for it! It is time to thrive instead of survive. You can believe in yourself because you have done the hard work and learned the lessons to make great decisions. It's all about finding magic in the everyday or creating something amazing out of what most people would overlook. Aries has a powerhouse mixture of creativity *and* follow-through. That is a magic combination. Aries are the experimental gardeners this year, putting their knowledge and unique world view into play to create a cornucopia of tasty delights.

Queen of Pentacles

Relationships

Sweet nostalgia will be hanging around for the next 12 months, Aries. Many of you have had a rocky few years in the romance department, but that energy is now leaving the scene. This will be a romantic time period for strong couples who have been together for a long time. Feelings will be flowing from the early days of your relationship. If you are single, you may meet someone from your past with whom you create a new partnership. It is more likely, though, that a new relationship will start that heals wounds from the past. Expect love to come knocking at your door! For some Aries this time period may bring the silent specter of unrequited love. Please be weary of 'the one that got away' interfering in your present relationship. If you are single, think twice about letting a troublemaker from the past back in. This person hasn't changed a bit, guaranteed!

6 of cups

Career/Projects

Ambition is charismatic and sexy. People who use it for the good of all are inspiring. Aries will have loads of it in 2014 and many of you may become mentors or trendsetters. Hold to your own vision and reach a well-defined goal. Your achievement will inspire others to action. You will teach through example. Do not censor your ideas with limiting beliefs because anything really *is* possible. The Magician is the first card in the entire tarot deck and it carries the qualities of fearlessness and idealism. A person harnessing this energy attracts to them whatever they need or want. Hot Damn!

Magician

Aries Monthly Meditations

January: It's a good month for a makeover! Get some new ideas and put them into action. You are able to make a plan and stick to it right now. Do it! If you don't want to get pregnant, be careful this month! If you want to start a new project, now is the perfect time.

February: Past actions will bring you good karma now. You may receive some unexpected good news stemming from a past situation. Be generous with compliments and kindness this month.

March: Decisiveness comes easily and moves things along. A trip could change the trajectory of your life. New technology or information will benefit you, so commit to learning it well.

April: Setting and achieving goals creates magic! Now is the time to make long range plans and put in the effort needed to achieve them. What do you want your life to look like in 5 years? Start working towards that vision today.

May: It is just about time for the fairytale to end with 'happily ever after'. The dragon has been slayed, the lessons learned. It is time to reap the rewards of your effort and rest up before the new story begins.

June: Being proactive about beginning something will pay off later. Any challenges you overcome on the new path will be absolutely worth it due to the success you achieve. Strength comes through adversity!

July: A vision quest could change your life! Don't ignore restlessness. Look within for the answers. If you change your inner world, the outer world will follow. Take a walk instead of watch a movie. Clear your mind space and inspiration will fill it.

August: Although it may feel counter intuitive, moving into the unknown is better than sticking with an unsatisfying situation. You may be giving a lot more out than you are receiving in return. Taking a risk for happiness will pay off.

September: It's a great time to get things done. The world is your oyster! Don't be controlling with others, just mind yourself. An entrepreneur may influence your life this month.

October: There is beauty everywhere, even in dark times. Train yourself to look for it. A life changing inspiration can hit at any time, be open to it. Understand that there is only one of you and you are beautiful!

November: You are on the verge of success! Your hard work will be recognized by others. Beware of 'imposter syndrome'. Nobody is making a mistake…you are the one they admire. You can handle anything that comes your way.

December: If you know what you want you will eventually get what you want. Pick up lucky pennies and wish upon a star! The universe is blessing you with gentle luck. A sense of excitement for the future enters the picture. You are blessed!

TAURUS

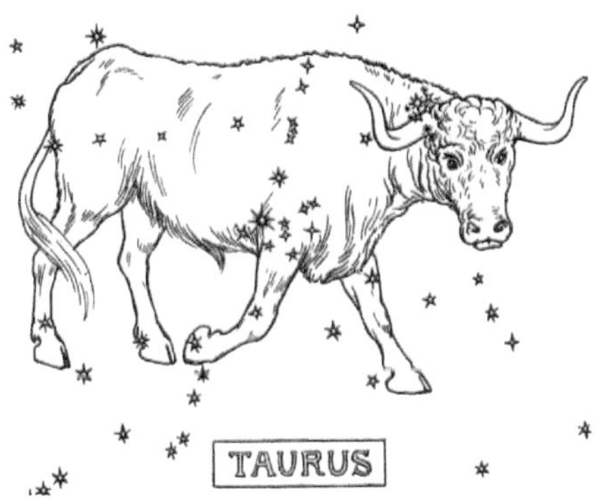

Overview

This year is about readjustment and being self-centered in the most glorious way. Many Tauruses are re-evaluating where they are going and some are even changing who they are and how they present themselves to the world. There is a sense of wanting to change everything! They are on a course correction, but it might be fun! Tauruses are excellent at building solid foundations…too good, sometimes. In 2014 many will want to tear down (or at least alter) what they have built because it has become too constrictive. *This is a spiritual situation.* Hang tight and see this time period as an evolution, not a revolution. Adjustment is necessary to prepare for the next era. Some Tauruses just want to stay on the 'change' plateau, where they don't have to make any heavy decisions. That is OK for awhile. But this can never be a permanent place for a Taurus; eventually they will need to rebuild the foundation. 2014 should be a very, very interesting time period for the Bull.

2 of Wands

Relationships

Relations with others should be harmonious and life giving this year. There will be an emphasis on groups, collectives and many different relationships. Partnerships will more likely be embedded in a community or found through friendships and social connections. Established couples will benefit from going out with others, rather than isolating themselves. Humans are social beings! A partner is wonderful, but can't fulfill every social and emotional need. Tauruses will feel this particularly strongly in 2014. It will benefit couples to support a Taurus partner who wants go out with friends or pursue a goal solo. Stretch your soul and widen your group of associates to enrich your reality this year.

3 of Cups

Career/Projects

Fresh ideas, projects or job locations will greet Taurus in 2014. A sense of optimism and clarity will roll in and add a sparkle to the workaday world. New opportunities will be around every corner…but only if you are ready for them! Just be careful not to bite off more than you can chew in your excitement, because eventually you may run out of energy to see your vision through to a successful end. As in the rest of life this year, it is a great time to incorporate others into making a concept reality. This may actually be a 'group' vision having to do with life-giving actions or art. Collectives, collaborations or mutual causes will carry more energy than a solo project.

Sun

Taurus Monthly Meditations

January: A charming person is going to enter your life and bring new ideas. Sometimes, but not always, this is someone who sweeps you off your feet and then disappears. Heed red flags if you think someone isn't being honest. This can be in love or business. Otherwise expect good news.

February: The difference between how you want things to be and how they really are is your main cause of misery. First try to change things for the better. If that doesn't work you must accept the situation as it is or leave it. The most painful, draining thing to do is *nothing.*

March: Transformation is at hand. Don't hold on to anything that is trying to leave your life. Just let go and don't panic! The sun will rise tomorrow. Loss at this time will lead to freedom later, particularly in relationships. Don't settle for less…true love is around the corner.

April: Freewill and luck intersect in an unforgettable way. Any effort put forth will be rewarded by a surprising turn of events. Expect the unexpected! In time you will understand exactly why everything happened the way it did.

May: It's a good month for a makeover! Get some new ideas and put them into action. You are able to make a plan and stick to it right now. Do it! If you don't want to get pregnant, be careful this month! If you want to start a new project, now is the perfect time.

June: An end is at hand. It's time to tie up loose ends, face the facts and call it a day. Don't stay here too long…it is only a temporary situation. A sense of liberation will soon replace your heavy heart. Delegate some responsibilities to others and spend some time on your own. It is time to follow your own inner light. Do you need to strike the match?

July: Salvage what you can and move on. You are not supposed to stay in a confusing or painful situation. Keep Moving! Direct communication may be tough, but it will transform everything for the better.

August: It is just about time for the fairytale to end with 'happily ever after'. The dragon has been slayed, the lessons learned. It is time to reap the rewards of your effort and rest up before the new story begins.

September: Give yourself credit for your awesomeness. Be proud of all that you've accomplished and realize that no matter what, you will always have yourself! Take responsibility for everything in your life…the good and bad. Keep it or throw it away…it's up to you. You don't owe anyone an explanation…ever!

October: A joyful experience is at hand. Gratitude is the key and the liberator. If you are single, a new relationship may be about to begin. If you are attached, a magical time period arrives. Share your wealth and time and it will come back tenfold.

November: It's time to talk about your ideas with others. Sharing hopes and dreams and plans will help them be realized. Sometimes talking is all it takes to start the ball rolling! Networking is more powerful than planning right now.

December: A difficult time period is coming to an end! Instead of asking 'Why did that happen to me?' just say 'Thank you it's over' and look to the future. Things will just keep getting better and better. You are on the road to recovery. Don't look back!

GEMINI

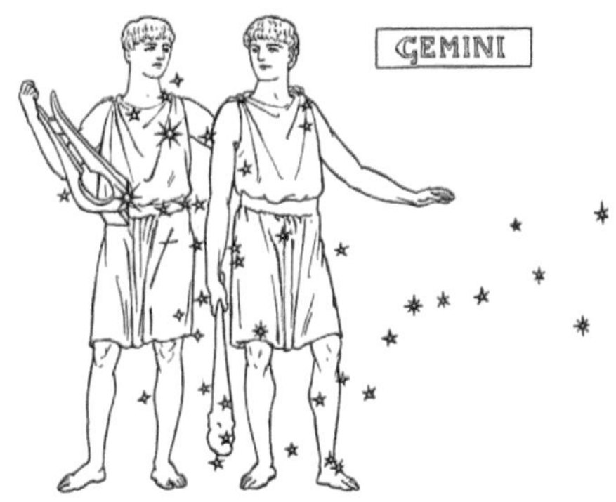

Overview

Opportunity is everywhere this year, arriving in different packages and by different means. Some situations will just drop into Gemini's lap and ask for a decision. Should you follow the new path or stick to the seemingly stable present reality? Other opportunities will be self-created from personal goals you have set. These created opportunities are very powerful and no less valuable than surprising 'lucky' breaks. Even if some of the ways you go about trying to achieve these ideals feels contrived, often times the magic happens on the other side of the effort. The universe will see your 'contrived' methods as effort nonetheless and reward you with an unmistakable response. Remember, you can't win the lottery without buying the ticket! The universe always sees sincere effort and reacts to it. Some opportunities may present themselves to you simply by you shifting your perspective. Choosing to believe that you are *never* stuck in any situation is enough to get the energy moving and new doors opening.

Multiverse

Relationships

Gemini, this is the year to assess your various relationships and decide which ones deserve priority. Many people will be asking for your attention in 2014 and you'll have to decide who gets it because there is only so much of you to go around! Surround yourself with loving, life-giving people and avoid spending time with *anyone* out of a sense of obligation or who isn't 100% trustworthy. In romantic relationships, this is the year of the Butterfly effect. Whether you are single or partnered, seemingly small occurrences can end up having a huge effect later. Don't underestimate the power of a glance, a loving gesture or a genuine smile…originating from you or the other person. There will be no 'coincidences' this year, only synchronicity.

2 of Pentacles

Career/Projects

There is a synergistic energy of new inspiration and fiery action in Gemini's professional life this year! Opportunities will be plentiful, with many of them self-made. You may develop a new passion for your work or suddenly find an exciting new career path. A sense of being in the right place at the right time will permeate Gemini's work world. Your sign is the visionary of the Zodiac, so use your inspiration to advance yourself in your career and financial life. This year, money will definitely follow ideas acted upon. Many Geminis may feel a spiritual force involved in what they are doing for a living.

Ace of Wands

Gemini Monthly Meditations

`January:` It's time to talk about your ideas with others. Sharing hopes and dreams and plans will help them be realized. Sometimes talking is all it takes to start the ball rolling! Networking is more powerful than planning right now.

`February:` At the 11th hour, when you've just about given up hope of getting what you want or need, it will come to you. You will experience a breakthrough in some aspect of your life that will be a great relief to you.

`March:` Take a risk for happiness! Security is important but it isn't more important than mystery. We need both in equal measure. Restlessness is a call from your soul to move in a new direction…without needing to know the outcome.

`April:` You are the creator of your own reality. Move forward with clarity and excitement and believe you can achieve whatever you set your mind on. Luckily you get what you settle for. What? That's right. If you don't like it, change it.

`May:` A significant relationship could develop or deepen. Commitment is key! What is your relationship to commitment? Does it make you feel safe or does it feel confining? Is it easy or hard to commit to yourself? Or another? Or your job? A situation is calling for your dedication and a small sacrifice will lead to long term happiness.

`June:` Don't be afraid to rock the boat. Move forward in a situation in spite of fears. Make a decision even if you don't want to. Remember that every time you point a finger at someone else, you have three fingers pointing back at yourself.

July: Salvage what you can and move on. You are not supposed to stay in a confusing or painful situation. Keep Moving! Direct communication may be tough, but it will transform everything for the better.

August: A difficult time period is coming to an end! Instead of asking 'Why did that happen to me?' just say 'Thank you it's over' and look to the future. Things will just keep getting better. You are on the road to recovery. Don't look back!

September: Any struggle or competition will develop qualities you can call on later. Overcoming adversity is great for your growth! Follow through until the end because the outcome will be worth the effort. Take an accepting and positive view of your situation. Being an Eyore won't help you or anyone around you.

October: Others see and respect your knowledge and experience. It may have been hard won, but it is all becoming worth it. Don't ignore red flags; your highly tuned bull$%#@ radar is spot on!

November: It's time to recalibrate! The scales are not balanced. Set boundaries with others so you can create more space for yourself. An unhappy you doesn't do anyone any good! You might come in to some money this month from an unexpected source.

December: You are never trapped. You always have freedom of choice. If you feel caught in a situation or habit, realize you have the power to free yourself. Your subconscious is powerful now…for better or worse. Creativity and passion live there, but so do jealousy and darker things. Try to be accepting of your imperfections. You aren't seeing yourself the way others are seeing you. You are on the verge of success! Your hard work will be recognized by others. Beware of 'imposter syndrome'. Nobody is making a mistake…you are the one they admire. You can handle anything that comes your way.

CANCER

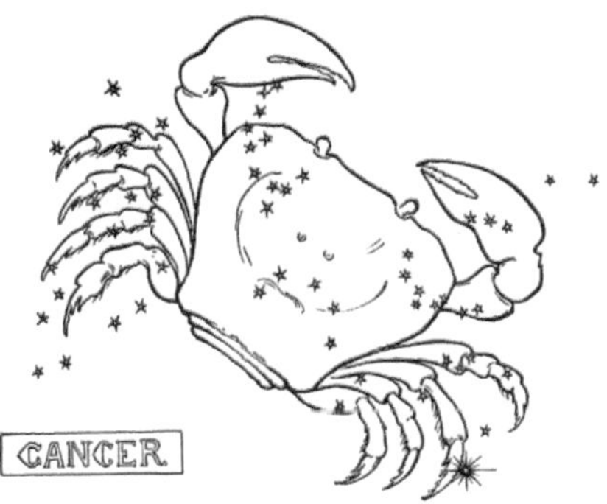

Overview

Many Cancers will be impatient this year! They are waiting for the results of a long term endeavor to come to fruition. This plan has taken a lot of energy and planning. Just hang in there. The universe always rewards effort. The outcome may not be exactly what you envisioned, but it will definitely be worth the effort! Sometimes things don't follow the timeline you set up, but if you know what you want and persevere you almost always get it! Many Cancers may feel that a better tomorrow is just around the corner…and it is! All the hard work will pay off shortly; you are in the time period right before big, positive changes take place. Take a deep breath and feel safe and happy that things are going in the right direction and you are doing a great job creating what you want.

7 of Pentacles

Relationships

'Separate but together' is the 2014 theme for Cancers already in a committed relationship. This is the normal state of affairs for certain signs that have a more independent love style; but for most water signs, Cancer being one, the *urge to merge* is the primary motivator. When Cancers fall in love, they love like motherf*****, so 'separate but together' doesn't really come naturally. Every relationship can benefit from both partners having independent interests and time apart. This will be extra true for Crabs this year. Don't panic! Trust in your relationship and your mate and go do something on your own, especially if it is personally meaningful. If you are single, this will be an especially fun year for dating where you feel comfortable with yourself and magnetic. Your choice in partners should be especially good because you will be more detached in love than usual, therefore you won't be inclined to ignore red flags or get involved in messy situations.

9 of Pentacles

Career/Projects

2014 holds the potential for experiencing a deeply meaningful connection to your means of livelihood. Any energy spent in this direction will be well rewarded. If you have been contemplating a new career direction that involves re-education, relocation or anything else that takes you out of your comfort zone but simultaneously makes you feel excited, this is the year to create a new work reality. If you are already in the field of your choice, it is time to take it up a notch. Don't just be good at what you do, be phenomenal. 2014 is not the year to stay detached from your 'work' (as you define it); it is the year to get emotionally invested in the most positive and fulfilling way.

2 of Cups

Cancer Monthly Meditations

January: The sudden revelation of a hidden truth could change everything. The time calls for the release of unbearable tension and/or situations. Fresh energy will follow the upheaval…like the blooming of desert flowers after a storm. A new source of income rolls in after the turbulence.

February: You are harnessing a lot of charisma right now. Use it! People will respond to your generosity and warmth. Give it all away freely and receive it back tenfold. You have the power of persuasion, use it with care!

March: At the 11th hour, when you've just about given up hope of getting what you want or need, it will come to you. You will experience a breakthrough in some aspect of your life that will be a great relief to you.

April: Get out and do something with others. Spend time doing what you care about. There are a million different way to make life better for everyone. Join others to create a better quality of life for yourself. Don't go solo now.

May: It's time to recalibrate! The scales are not balanced. Set boundaries with others so you can create more space for yourself. An unhappy you doesn't do anyone any good! You might come in to some money this month from an unexpected source.

June: Something that you really want is going to fall into your lap. The trick about your wish coming true is *knowing* what you want. You can't get what you want if you don't know what you want. Trust that things will work out, even if you don't know exactly *how.*

July: Transformation is at hand. Don't hold on to anything that is trying to leave your life. Just let go and don't panic! The sun will rise tomorrow. Loss at this time will lead to freedom later! What would you do if this were you last week on earth?

August: Don't be afraid to rock the boat. Move forward in a situation in spite of fears. Make a decision even if you don't want to. Remember that every time you point a finger at someone else, you have three fingers pointing back at yourself.

September: Joyfully trust your own counsel. Other people's advice should be taken with a grain of salt. They may care about you, but your growth and new energy may be threatening to them on some level.

October: Just keep showing up and you will reach your goal. That's it. 90% of success comes through perseverance. Discipline yourself now and enjoy expansive freedom later!

November: Follow the moral high ground now. Use your higher self to make decisions and don't compromise yourself or your plans. Be the leader in an ambiguous situation. Raise someone up rather than let them drag you down.

December: You are the creator of your own reality. Move forward with clarity and excitement and believe you can achieve whatever you set your mind to. Luckily you get what you settle for. What? That's right. If you don't like it, change it.

LEO

Overview

2014 will bring Leos calm conditions that will be especially noticeable to those who have gone through tumultuous times in the last few years. Circumstances will continually lighten throughout the year bringing a sense of ease and flow. Hard lessons learned will bring rewards as balance is restored. It will be more beneficial to look towards the future and say 'Thank You!' that you are out of a difficult situation, rather than looking backwards and asking 'Why Me'? You may never know why things were so difficult so don't stay there emotionally. Gratitude for what you have now will bring you more to be grateful for. A sense of clarity about the future will visit many Leos. You are on the road to recovery of what was lost, but in new territory and with a sparkling clean lens of perception.

6 of Swords

Relationships

Taking care of practical matters in a relationship will lead to magical moments later! 2014 will be a great year to set solid foundations that will allow partners freedom in the future. Life isn't a movie where only the exciting bits of existence are highlighted. There are times when we must work hard, discipline ourselves, make sacrifices for long term goals and just have down time. This side of existence will be highlighted in Leo relationships this year, but it won't be drudgery! Working together for a shared goal will be extremely satisfying, especially if the end result is life altering. Mutual effort toward a common dream, starting a physical fitness regime together or saving money like rock stars will pay off in the future and many Leos may embark on a new financial adventure with a partner. The omens look good for this. If single, you may meet someone doing something totally mundane, like working or shopping. You may end up with a stable partner who wants a commitment and who will benefit you financially.

Ace of Pentacles

Career/Projects

It is time to prioritize your life and figure out where work fits in on your personal satisfaction list. If your job is at the very bottom, but it is taking up all your time, 2014 is the year to start planning for a change. Your perception of your situation is very important this year. Really think about what is *useful* for you to believe in regards to making money. Is it more useful to believe that you are trapped or that you have choice. If you are feeling stressed out it may be time to delegate responsibility to others. Burn out is possible, but not imminent. Some Leos may be at the end of a long project or about to finally receive an educational degree or certification. If this is you, know that you are just about to cross the finish line. Please take care of yourself in the meantime, until you receive your well earned booty .

10 of Wands

Leo Monthly Meditations

January: A situation is changing. You may have started it, but now it has a life of its own. Just ride it out to the end. All things happen for a reason. Stagnant situations are breaking up to be reformed or released.

February: You are in a waiting period. Use it to shore up your reserves for the next move. Beware of 'drift'. You could stay in this situation indefinitely. It will take intention and action to get what you want.

March: You are never trapped in a situation. There is always a choice and a chance. It is time to switch your perspective and take total responsibility for your happiness. The problem is with others at this time so remove yourself from their sphere of influence. Playing the victim now will be your downfall later.

April: An end is at hand. It's time to tie up loose ends, face the facts and call it a day. A sense of liberation will soon replace your heavy heart or lingering sadness. Delegate some responsibilities to others. Being controlling will not help you.

May: Freewill and luck intersect in an unforgettable way. Any effort put forth will be rewarded by a surprising turn of events. Expect the unexpected! In time you will understand exactly why everything happened the way it did.

June: Please have patience! You have done the hard work of laying foundations and now you must wait for everything to come together. 'Build it and they will come'! …but not always immediately!

July: It's time to talk about your ideas with others. Sharing hopes and dreams and plans will help them be realized. Sometimes talking is all it takes to start the ball rolling! Networking is more powerful than planning right now. It's party time!

August: It's a good month for a makeover! Get some new ideas and put them into action. You are able to make a plan and stick to it right now. Do it! If you don't want to get pregnant, be careful this month! If you want to start a new project, now is the perfect time.

September: Get out and do something with others. Spend time doing what you care about? There are a million different way to make life better for everyone. Join others to create a better quality of life for yourself. Don't go solo now.

October: You are the creator of your own reality. Move forward with clarity and excitement and believe you can achieve whatever you set your mind to. Luckily you get what you settle for. What? That's right. If you don't like it, change it.

November: Have courage right now! Don't waste time on being defensive; just live your life in the most amazing way possible. Draw a line in the sand and state your beliefs with conviction! You have more of an advantage than you think you do.

December: At the 11th hour, when you've just about given up hope of getting what you want or need, it will come to you. You will experience a breakthrough in some aspect of your life that will be a great relief to you.

VIRGO

Overview

Many Virgos will be crossing into a victorious new reality this year. Success is imminent, but the degree of it depends on how hard you have worked in the past. A certain degree of fame (or notoriety!) may even come your way. Others will take notice of your efforts or product and show appreciation. Lucky surprises will drop from the heavens all year! Stay open and get into the flow of life. Don't isolate yourself or put a lot of energy into trying to guarantee particular outcomes. This will drain your luck. Having fun and networking with others will bring more success than buckling down and putting your nose to the grindstone. You have already put in a ton of effort towards your goal, so now is the time to enjoy what you have been working towards. 2014 will be a year of receiving what you have earned.

6 of Wands

Relationships

Virgos may worry, but they put their anxiety to good use. They use the energy to get things done and keep their life in order. This trait is good for business but not so good for the variables of love. If you are in a solid relationship, don't let your own personal need for control bleed over into your relationship. Relaxing, being flexible and trusting the other is the key to happiness! Stop torturing yourself and try to look at your relationships with a more detached view. You'll have a lot more fun and an easier time in love if you do. If you are a single Virgo, 2014 could very well bring you a paramour who sweeps you off your feet! Enjoy! But remember that 'charm' is a verb and red flags are real this year, especially if you sense someone is commitment phobic or has intimacy issues. Just stay alert and don't let a crazy maker in to your inner life.

9 of Swords/Knight of Cups

Career/Projects

This is a fabulous year for beginning a new phase in your career life. The potential for a massive breakthrough is huge! Many Virgos are finally going to have career options available after a prolonged period of being in a 'job desert' or a stagnant situation. It's time to say 'good-bye' to desperation and 'hello' to inspiration! 2014 is a great year to breakout on your own or with others into a new reality. The energy surrounding an inspired idea is full of raw power. Some Virgos may receive inspiration like a bolt of lightning while others will move with a steady yet powerful energy toward an already established goal. Either way, the potent equation of *idea + action* will carry Virgos far this year.

Ace of Wands

Virgo Monthly Meditations

January: You may be starting a new job or a project that will bring in money later. Dedicate yourself 100% to your work and the payoff will be huge! It's not time for you to be the 'expert' in a situation. You need to listen and learn and be receptive now.

February: A fog has lifted and now the new day is bright! You can see everything clearly from a bird's eye view and this lifts your spirits. Even if there are some challenges ahead, at least you can see them and prepare. Have fun, get excited and plan for the best.

March: You could be involved in a situation that is attractive but dangerous. If you choose to stay keep your eyes wide open. In the end it will be worthwhile if you learn the lessons that life wants to teach you. Don't be afraid to take a leadership position now.

April: A joyful experience is at hand. Gratitude is the key and the liberator. If you are single, a new relationship may be about to begin. Share your wealth and time and it will come back tenfold.

May: It is time to be an activist for the most important cause in your life…your own happiness. Even if you are scared to stand up for yourself, do it. Remember that you don't owe *anyone* any explanations, ever.

June: Be open to receiving messages. Look for answers in unlikely places. You may be in the beginning stage of trying to make an idea real or breaking a bad habit. The outlook is good! Keep your plans in the forefront and conserve your energy because you are vulnerable to being sidetracked!

July: Emotional balance is easy to achieve. Conflicts will be resolved easily and quickly. Love with one other person is satisfying on a very deep level. A tender, loving union may start or be renewed.

August: It's time to talk about your ideas with others. Sharing hopes and dreams and plans will help them be realized. Sometimes talking is all it takes to start the ball rolling! Networking is more powerful than planning right now. It's party time!

September: Take a risk for happiness! Security is important but it isn't more important than mystery. We need both in equal measure. Restlessness is a call from your soul to move in a new direction…without needing to know the outcome.

October: Joyfully trust your own counsel. Other people's advice should be taken with a grain of salt. They may care about you, but your growth and new energy may be threatening to them on some level.

November: It's time to recalibrate! The scales are not balanced. Set boundaries with others so you can create more space for yourself. An unhappy you doesn't do anyone any good! You might come in to some money this month from an unexpected source.

December: You have the ability to create a secure present and future. Make sure you aren't clinging to situations or things that are actually holding you back. Sometimes you have to exchange the known for the unknown in order to grow.

LIBRA

Overview

This year will be about creating comfort and future security. Many Librans will be establishing a home or buying one and some may be creating a family…literally or figuratively. Don't waste time by not having an agenda. Planning for the long term and intentionally directing energy and money will yield massive returns later. Many of you are about to cross a threshold into a new era that will be full of foundation building. The sturdier your platform is built now, the more freedom you will have later and the more people you will be able to support. Seize the day…but do it responsibly and do it with others! Rope new and old friends into your master plan, be inclusive rather than exclusive and remember…the more the merrier. Don't try to control situations, just aim for your goals with flexibility and enthusiasm and take your loved ones with you.

10 of Pentacles

Relationships

In 2014 Librans will get what they give in love and relationships. Karma will be quick and impossible to miss. It will be as if the universe is using the people in your life like crystal clear mirrors, reflecting your actions back to you. This may be a wonderful experience or a challenging situation. You can decide what experiences you draw in through your actions. A primary relationship will probably go through significant changes…this could be moving into significant commitment or splitting for good. If you are a single Libra, any energy you put into finding love will be returned to you in equal measure. If you sit at home nothing will happen, so get out there if you want a relationship.

Justice

Career/Projects

The best way to navigate work this year is with your intuition! If you are an artist you will be able to pull up some fascinating imagery and inspiration from dreams and altered states. All Librans should listen to their dreams this year, even when it comes to life-path or career questions. A dream journal would be a great tool to use in getting answers to some of 2014's questions. If you aren't one hundred percent sure about a decision, either don't make it yet (you need more information) or rely on gut feelings and intuition rather than logic. If you run into any quandaries at work, chances are it involves bigger picture issues that you aren't aware of. Stay calm and work on your end of things. Don't try to force a situation, because it may backfire. Your hunches will probably be right, though, and creativity will be high.

Moon

Libra Monthly Meditations

January: Sadness over a difficult situation will start to fade. Delays are in your favor. It's the dark before the dawn. Beware of a threesome or troubles coming in threes. You are the creator of your own reality. Move forward with clarity and excitement and believe you can achieve whatever you set your mind to. Luckily, you get what you settle for. What? That's right. If you don't like it, change it.

February: You are never trapped in a situation. There is always a choice and a chance. It is time to switch your perspective and take total responsibility for your happiness. The problem is with others at this time so remove yourself from their sphere of influence if possible. Playing the victim now will be your downfall later. It's time to recalibrate! The scales are not balanced. Set boundaries with others so you can create more space for yourself. An unhappy you doesn't do anyone any good! You might come in to some money this month from an unexpected source.

March: Excitement is building! Make sure you know what you want, because the smallest step you take towards your goal will quickly gain momentum. Obstacles will be removed or bypassed and synchronicities will multiply. Be careful what you wish for!

April: It's a good month for a makeover! Get some new ideas and put them into action. You are able to make a plan and stick to it right now. Do it! If you don't want to get pregnant, be careful this month! If you want to start a new project, now is the perfect time.

May: Any struggle or competition will bring out your best qualities. Follow through until the end because the outcome will be worth the effort. At the 11th hour, when you've just about given up hope of getting what you want or need, it will come to you. You will experience a breakthrough in some aspect of your life that will be a great relief to you.

June: Salvage what you can and move on. You are not supposed to stay in a confusing or painful situation. Keep Moving! Direct communication may be tough, but it will transform everything for the better.

July: Don't reinvent the wheel! Learn from people or groups who have gone there before you. Join first then break off on your own. If you have life experience, share it!

August: Transformation is at hand. Don't hold on to anything that is trying to leave your life. Just let go and don't panic! The sun will rise tomorrow. Loss at this time will lead to freedom later! What would you do today if it were your last day?

September: Get out and do something with others. What do you care about? There are a million different ways to make life better for everyone. Join others to make a better world and a better quality of life for yourself. Don't go solo now.

October: It's time to take a risk for happiness. Security is important but it isn't more important than mystery. We need both in equal measure. Restlessness is a call from your soul to move in a new direction…without having to know the outcome.

November: It's time to talk about your ideas with others. Sharing hopes and dreams and plans will help them be realized. Sometimes talking is all it takes to start the ball rolling! Networking is more powerful than planning right now. It's party time!

December: The karmic wheel is turning. You are reaping what you've sown. Intention is everything now. You can't hide the truth from the universe, even if you can cloak it from others…or even yourself!

SCORPIO

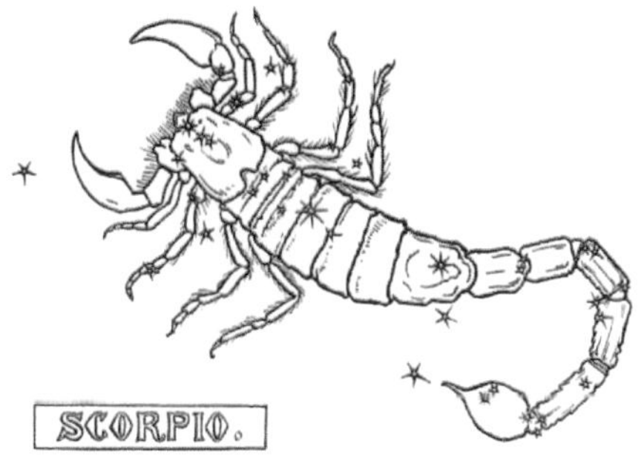

Overview

This year Scorpios will be able to accomplish anything, especially if their motivation is soul deep! Many will find themselves hyper focused on a goal, held in the grip of an 'enlightened' obsession. The connection between physical, emotional and mental health will be especially apparent now. Taking care of your body will create mental clarity and a positive mind state and help you get into the flow of creative production. Your inspired action may influence others who end up putting you into a leadership position! It's time to take your skill level from 'good' to 'phenomenal'. What would you have to do to accomplish that? This year could be a real game changer if you dedicate yourself to your highest potential. Good luck will be easy to come by and people will be helpful.

Magician

Relationships

Scorpios have a reputation for being passionate to a fault and having a vindictive side, so it is interesting when your Scorpio friend or colleague portrays none of these traits! That is because Scorpio's shadowy and emotional side usually only comes out in intimate relationships. This year many of you will get clear about past relationship mistakes and take action to correct them. Wonderful! This will completely change your romantic luck, bringing in a fresh energy and new possibilities. Don't be afraid to show vulnerability and jump into a relationship with both feet! Taking risks for love is where your luck lies this year. Being hot and cold will backfire, as will any manipulative actions or half-hearted gestures. This is true for single or committed Scorpios. Have fun and deal with your fears on your own time, don't take them out on others! Coincidences will have meaning and may change your fate in 2014. Bon Chance!

Queen of Swords/Fool

Career/Projects

Being proactive about learning new skills or developing a new plan of action will be highly profitable this year. If you are self-employed invest in an image overhaul or new avenues of promotion. If you work for someone else, take the initiative to get more accreditation or go the extra mile on a project. This is good advice for any time, but it will be especially important this year, as the times are re-adjusting and progressing especially fast after years of stagnation.

Initiative is magnetic and focused energy is sexy. Others will be attracted to your ambition and when push comes to shove in the second half of 2014, you'll be a shining star.

Judgment

Scorpio Monthly Meditations

`January:` Some experts say that only 7% of communication is verbal. That leaves 93% to what we call 'intuition'. Intuition is a massive, powerful and trustworthy information machine. Just because it lives outside the five senses doesn't mean it doesn't exist. Believe in it. Use it.

`February:` A significant relationship could develop or deepen. Commitment is key! What is your relationship to commitment? Does it make you feel safe or does it feel confining? Is it easy or hard to commit to yourself? Or another? Or your job? A situation is calling for your dedication and a small sacrifice will lead to long term happiness.

`March:` An end is at hand. It's time to tie up loose ends, face the facts and call it a day. A sense of liberation will soon replace your heavy heart or lingering sadness. Delegate some responsibilities to others. Being controlling will not help you.

`April:` It is time to be an activist for the most important cause in your life…your own happiness. Even if you are scared to stand up for yourself, do it. Remember that you don't owe *anyone* any explanations, ever.

`May:` Any struggle or competition will bring out your best qualities. Follow through until the end because the outcome will be worth the effort.

`June:` Emotional balance is easy to achieve. Conflicts will be resolved easily and quickly. Love with one other person is satisfying on a very deep level. A tender, loving union may start or be renewed

`July:` Don't be afraid to rock the boat. Move forward in a situation in spite of fears. Make a decision even if you don't want to.

Remember that every time you point a finger at someone else, you have three fingers pointing back at yourself.

August: Are you trying to break into a new field? One of the best ways to do this is to become an apprentice. Working for little or no money now is actually a free education and an investment in your future. Don't be afraid to be a beginner!

September: Please have patience! You have done the hard work of laying foundations and now you must wait for everything to come together. 'Build it and they will come'! …but not always immediately!

October: You are in a waiting period. Use it to shore up your reserves for the next move. Beware of 'drift'. You could stay in this situation indefinitely. It will take intention and action to get what you want.

November: A situation is changing. You may have started it, but now it has a life of its own. Just ride it out to the end. All things happen for a reason. Stagnant situations are breaking up to be reformed or released.

December: Be open to flashes of inspiration. Switching up your usual routine will bring fresh energy into your life. Ask for divine inspiration if you are feeling stuck in something. A great idea will come to you, but it is up to you to act on it. In love, this is a very passionate time.

SAGITTARIUS

Overview

Things will flow easily and fall into place without a lot of effort in 2014! The variables of life have really taken Sagittarians for a wild ride the last few years and now there is a place to rest. The year will ask you to prioritize 'being and experiencing' over 'producing' or pushing an agenda. If given enough space, you could have a creative breakthrough! Travelling or putting yourself in new, exciting environments will stir your creative soul. People will be drawn to your kindheartedness this year, rather than your fiery unpredictability. All humans have been through the ringer lately and are just looking for some love! Follow your feelings rather than your intellect and it will change the trajectory of your life. Seize the day, Sag!

Empress

Relationships

The end of a relationship journey will be reached this year. Either a couple in crisis will resolve the issues in a *very* satisfactory way or a partnership will end that has run its natural course. If you are a single Sagittarius you may find true love and a committed relationship in 2014. Each of these scenarios is different, but the energetic pattern is similar; Sagittarian relationship status is going to change. The times are calling for a 'New Day' in the Sagittarians' relationship realm. There are no mistakes in 2014, everything will be happening for a reason. It is a season of re-adjustment and by the end of the year things should resolve into 'happily ever after'…or the closest proximity to that state possible! Travel will add a magical twist to love, especially if it is a place you have never been.

Universe

Career/Projects

In the world of work, it is the year of the Sag! Don't squelch your ideas in 2014. Research and present your concepts to others. Your ideas will be met with enthusiasm and may bring a big boost to your reputation…and pocketbook! Bringing new elements into an existing project or presenting a streamlined or creative blueprint for your workplace will inspire everyone. Don't be afraid to be a beginner. Believe in your ideas, even if you aren't 100% sure how you are going to achieve them. Your inspired vision will inspire others, so if you can't do it alone pull in someone who has skills you don't. People will want to work with you this year. If you are trying to decide between a couple of different positions, take the job that offers the most room for growth, even if it starts out at a lower pay scale. You will earn much more later on!

Page of Wands

Sagittarius Monthly Meditations

January: Excitement is building! Make sure you know what want, because the smallest step you take towards your goal will quickly gain momentum. Obstacles will be removed or bypassed and synchronicities will multiply. Be careful what you wish for!

February: Past actions will bring you good karma now. You may receive some unexpected good news stemming from a past situation. Be generous with compliments and kindness this month.

March: A charming person is going to enter your life and bring new ideas. Sometimes, but not always, this is someone who sweeps you off your feet and then disappears. Heed red flags if you think someone isn't being honest. This can be in love or business. Otherwise expect good news.

April: Being proactive about beginning something will pay off later. Any challenges you overcome on the new path will be absolutely worth it due to the success you achieve. Overcoming adversity is a psychic workout.

May: You may feel more sensitive than usual. This is good! Let your emotions run the show for awhile. Hiding your feelings will cause more harm than good. In fact hiding your emotions may be a lie of omission under the circumstances.

June: An end is at hand. It's time to tie up loose ends, face the facts and call it a day. A sense of liberation will soon replace your heavy heart or lingering sadness. Delegate some responsibilities to others. Being controlling will not help you. Things are rearranging themselves and you need to be patient. Don't force any decisions right now. Look at situations in your life from a new angle. Just remember everything happens for a reason.

July: Sadness over a difficult situation will start to fade. Delays are in your favor. It's the dark before the dawn. Beware of a threesome or trouble coming in threes. You are in the grip of an unfounded fear or are experiencing anxiety about your future. Keep your thoughts in the present and wait for things to work themselves out. Everything will be ok.

August: It is time for a vision quest! Look within for the answers. If you change your inner world, the outer world will follow. Take a walk instead of watch a movie. Clear your mind space and inspiration will fill it.

September: A significant relationship could develop or deepen. Commitment is key! What is your relationship to commitment? Does it make you feel safe or does it feel confining? Is it easy or hard to commit to yourself? Or another? Or your job? A situation is calling for your dedication and a small sacrifice will lead to long term happiness.

October: People who are in love with their own life continuously create magic. Figure out what would make you love your life and take action! Use all your resources and intelligence, and fate will be on your side.

November: You feel oppressed by circumstances in your life. Lighten the load by delegating responsibilities and taking less on. Things will get easier if you don't try to do it all. You don't need to carry the world on your shoulders, get some help. Things will lighten up soon.

December: If you know what you want you will eventually get what you want. Pick up lucky pennies and wish upon a star! The universe is blessing you with gentle luck. A sense of excitement for the future enters the picture. You are blessed!

CAPRICORN

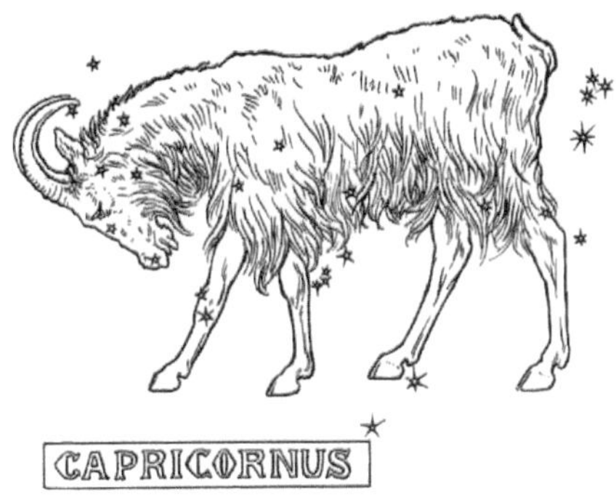

Overview

2014 will be a great year to make new friends and deepen bonds with those who are already in your life. If you are a single Capricorn you may enter into a deeply significant love relationship in the next twelve months. Drama will be at a minimum and connection will be easy. This ease of relating will be a welcome break for many Capricorns who were affected by their ruling planet, Saturn, going through the house of relationship for the past few years. That transit is over and the new energy is here. Hopefully most of you have a select few friends with whom to go into the new era. Let a friendship go if it is time to move on, because the void will be filled with fresh faces. Overall other people should be friendly, helpful and fun and life will be wonderfully satisfying this year.

Ace of Cups

Relationships

The past is done and cannot be undone! Focus your energy on what you want to bring in, rather than on what you are afraid of happening. Your worst fears are most likely not going to happen…in fact the exact opposite may come to pass in 2014! So what do you want to manifest in love and relationship? Getting clear on what you desire is critical to achieving it. You can have what you want…if you believe you can. Capricorns will make better and healthier decisions this year if they come from a place of hope and trust in life rather than fear or jealousy. Try to be understanding rather than controlling (a behavior coming out of past hurt). If a situation isn't working, take action. Don't just sit in the discomfort and emotional turmoil. There is a solution and a beautiful future. You will get what you want!

9 of Swords/Emperor

Career/Projects

Wow! Capricorns may have so many ideas about what they want to pursue or create in 2014 that they almost feel paralyzed! That is a blessed dilemma! Many of you may fear that choosing one path necessarily closes off another path. *This isn't true.* You can always change your mind! (Only dead people don't change their minds.) This is a hard lesson for the earth signs, who have the most amazing follow-through, but sometimes don't know when to release a situation. Sometimes Capricorns will stay in an unsatisfying position or push a project through to the very end, even at great disadvantage to themselves. Quitting and changing paths is not a sin, in fact it may be the best decision under certain circumstances. So make a decision and go for it! If it doesn't feel right change course. It isn't your business what anyone thinks of you.

7 of Cups

Capricorn Monthly Meditations

January: You don't have all the information! Hold off on reacting or deciding a little longer. Either you need to do more research about a pending situation, or get the full truth out of someone who has been less than forthcoming. Dreams are powerful now.

February: Joyfully trust your own counsel. Other people's advice should be taken with a grain of salt. They may care about you, but your growth and new energy may be threatening to them on some level.

March: Something that you really want is going to fall into your lap. The trick about your wish coming true is *knowing* what you want. You can't get what you want if you don't know what you want. Trust even if you don't know exactly *how*.

April: This is a time period full of love, joy and connection. You are finally going to find or reconnect to your community. A feeling of being at home will enter your life. You may enter into a relationship that is part of a bigger community, rather than being an isolated twosome.

May: Life might feel less than stellar right now. Are you feeling lonely or lost? You don't have to stay here. Hard times are not supposed to be permanent and constant difficulty is not your destiny. The key is to change your outlook. What you believe deep down is what you end up creating outside of yourself. Change your beliefs and everything will rearrange itself around you.

June: There is beauty everywhere, even in dark times. Train yourself to look for it. A life changing inspiration can hit at any moment, be open to it. Understand that there is only one of you and you are beautiful!

`July:` You are in a waiting period. Use it to shore up your reserves for the next move. Beware of 'drift'. You could stay in this situation indefinitely. It will take intention and action to get what you want.

`August:` New income streams are revealing themselves. Go for it. Starting a new physical discipline will have multiple benefits: physical, emotional and social. Try something new that you always wondered about.

`September:` Have courage right now! Don't waste time on being defensive; just live your life in the most amazing way possible. Draw a line in the sand and state your beliefs with conviction! You have more of an advantage than you think you do.

`October:` Putting space between you and your boring, everyday responsibilities will pay off extravagantly. It's a great time to go into self-imposed exile in order to refill the emotional and creative well.

`November:` Some experts say that only 7% of communication takes place with words. That leaves 93% to what we call 'intuition'. Intuition is a massive, powerful and trustworthy information machine. Just because it lives outside the five senses doesn't mean it doesn't exist. Believe in it. Use it.

`December:` You may be starting a new job or a project that will bring in money later. Dedicate yourself 100% and the payoff will be huge! It's not time for you to be the 'expert' in a situation. You need to listen and learn and be receptive now.

AQUARIUS

Overview

Many Aquarians will have important revelations in 2014. If this new information gets used, rather than ignored, it could be life changing! A secret revealed or a shared truth may answer a question that has been haunting you. This mystery may be outside of yourself, involving one or more people, or t it could be an inner truth that you finally face and integrate. Pluto, the planet of hardcore transition, is in the house of the unconscious for all Aquarians. The next few years may bring life changing insights and freedom from the past. If you come into a situation this year where your gut says one thing but your mind says another, follow your intuition. You don't have all the intel, but your hunches will be correct. Write down your dreams and take them seriously because they are messengers of truth this year. *Moon*

Relationships

A fresh, new energy enters Aquarian relationships in 2014. Romantic, friendly and family relationships will all be affected. If you are a single Aquarian it will be an easy year to be social and meet someone. The energy is lightening up around interpersonal connections after 3 hard astrological years. Have fun and cultivate optimism and before you know it love will cross your path. This is also true for Aquarians in a long-term relationship. A sense of connection and contentment comes with new clarity about old issues and patterns. Honesty and directness will change the path of many relationships this year. Wherever TRUTH leads, regardless of the outcome, it is the right path. Manipulation will be difficult in the next 12 months due to the bright and constant energy of the cosmic forces. Subterfuge needs dark places for its very existence and there won't be many in 2014!

Sun

Career/Projects

2014 will be an excellent year for getting recognition for your work. Some Aquarians might even have a brush with fame! Many Aquarians will be pushing through into a new level of success, but it will be a well earned blessing! A deeply satisfying sense of accomplishment will come with the promotion, degree or whatever form the success comes cloaked in. If you are in the last stretch of a competition, don't stop! Persevere to the end because it will be worth it. A new reality is at hand and within reach. You are a winner! Believe it and then you will see it. Try not to be impatient or irritable. Success is imminent, so just have as good a time as possible while you wait for it to arrive.

6 of Wands

Aquarius Monthly Meditations

January: Salvage what you can and move on. You are not supposed to stay in a confusing or painful situation. Keep Moving! Direct communication may be tough, but it will transform everything for the better.

February: A situation is changing. You may have started it, but now it has a life of its own. Just ride it out to the end. All things happen for a reason. Stagnant situations are breaking up to be reformed or released.

March: There is beauty everywhere, even in dark times. Train yourself to look for it. A life changing inspiration can hit at any time, be open to it. Understand that there is only one of you and you are beautiful!

April: Past actions will bring you fabulous karma now. You may receive some unexpected good news stemming from a past situation. Be generous with compliments and kind gestures this month.

May: Don't get caught in the grip of drift! Making no decisions *is* a decision. The path of least resistance leads to hell. Daydreaming is awesome…if it leads to action. Getting caught in dreamy twilight thought patterns…especially about romance, is just escapism.

June: It's a great time to get things done. The world is your oyster! Don't be controlling with others, just worry about your own actions. An entrepreneur may influence your life this month.

July: People who are in love with their own life create magic constantly. Figure out what would make you love your life and take action! Use all your resources and intelligence and fate will be on your side.

August: The sudden revelation of a hidden truth could change everything. The time calls for the release of unbearable tension or situations. Fresh energy will follow the upheaval…like the blooming of desert flowers after a storm. Being proactive about beginning something will pay off later. Any challenge you overcome on the new path will be worth it due to the success you achieve. Strength comes through overcoming adversity!

September: You are able to manifest anything you put your mind to. People will be amazed at how much you get done with seemingly little effort! Stay flexible to keep life balanced.

October: An inspiration may hit you like a rogue wave this month. It will not be ignored! Value yourself and your own worth enough to prioritize it.

November: Putting space between you and your boring, everyday responsibilities will pay off extravagantly. It's a great time to go into self-imposed exile in order to refill the emotional and creative well.

December: You don't have all the information! Hold off on reacting or deciding a little longer. Either you need to do more research about a pending situation, or get the full truth out of someone who has been less than forthcoming. Dreams are powerful now. You are harnessing a lot of charisma, so use it! People will respond to your generosity and warmth. Give it all away freely and receive it back tenfold. You have the power of persuasion, use it with care!

PISCES

Overview

This year Pisces will be busy managing several situations at once! Luckily this sign is a jack of all trades, being the last sign of the Zodiac and containing all other signs in it. The pace of life may feel crazy at times, but it will be exciting and there will be a lot of fun energy zooming around. You will be able to successfully pursue two goals at the same time this year, but take care of yourself so you dson't burn out. Several situations will occur that have contradictory energies, but the way you deal with them will impress others and teach you something about yourself. By the end of 2014 you will feel a true sense of accomplishment and a new sense of what you are truly capable of.

2 of Pentacles

Relationships

2014 will be a powerful year for relationships! Many Pisces will be starting a new phase in an existing relationship, spurred on by a newly revealed truth. Single Pisces may get swept up in an unexpected romantic development and find themselves miles off shore, carried away by a current that is deceptively strong. The energy around interconnection will be impossible to miss and action will be called for. Proactively dealing with situations, stating your truth or nipping things in the bud will guarantee success later. Just rolling with things may get you in over your head! Overall it should be a good year, but don't be afraid to draw a line in the sand if you need to. Boundaries are good for everyone!

Ace of Swords

Career/Projects

Your inner vision will be strong this year. Don't keep the information to yourself even if you aren't sure what others will think. Your ideas are valuable, insightful and worth sharing. Don't be surprised if others love what you present and want to act on your ideas! There are many different ways this can happen, so be careful about immediately reacting to or accepting an offer or proposition. Someone might even 'steal' your idea! If you work for someone else, you may have to call attention to the fact that you have grown past your current position and want to move up the ladder. Call attention to yourself and your strengths (don't be afraid to do some self-promotion!) and others will respond. It will be a good year if you are in a creative field or in the intuitive arts. Let yourself daydream, Pisces, it won't be a waste of time!

Page of Cups/7 of Pentacles

Pisces Monthly Meditations

January: Setting and achieving goals creates magic! Now is the time to make long range plans and put the effort in to achieve them. What do you want your life to look like in 5 years? Start working towards that vision today.

February: It's a great time to get things done. The world is your oyster! Don't be controlling with others, just concern yourself with your own behavior. An entrepreneur may influence your life this month.

March: Excitement is building! Make sure you know what want, because the smallest step you take towards your goal will quickly gain momentum. Obstacles will be removed or bypassed and synchronicities will multiply. Be careful what you wish for!

April: You are never trapped in a situation. There is always a choice and a chance. It is time to switch your perspective and take total responsibility for your happiness. The problem is with others at this time so remove yourself from their sphere of influence. Playing the victim now may feel satisfying, but it won't get you what you want.

May: Things will get easier if you don't try to do it all. You feel oppressed by circumstances in your life. Lighten the load by delegating responsibilities to others. You don't need to carry the world on your shoulders, get some help.

June: Pursue long term goals rather than getting sidetracked by short term gratification. Freedom lies on the other side of discipline. At the present time, the path of least resistance leads you astray. You are in the driver's seat of your life.

July: You are the creator of your own reality. Move forward with clarity and excitement and believe you can achieve whatever you set your mind on. Luckily you get what you settle for. What? That's right. If you don't like the way things are, change them.

August: Have courage right now! Don't waste time on being defensive; just live your life in the most amazing way possible. Draw a line in the sand and state your beliefs with conviction! You have more of an advantage than you think you do.

September: It is time for a vision quest! Look within for the answers. If you change your inner world, the outer world will follow. Take a walk instead of watch a movie. Clear your mind space and inspiration will fill it.

October: You are in a waiting period. Use it to shore up your reserves for the next move. Beware of 'drift'. You could stay in this situation indefinitely. It will take intention and action to get what you want.

November: Don't reinvent the wheel! Learn from people or groups who have gone there before you. Join first then break off on your own. If you have life experience, share it!

December: Certain parts of your life are wrapping up to make room for the new. You don't need to force anything, just be patient. Don't do the same things if you want a different outcome!

www.ingramcontent.com/pod-product-compliance
Ingram Content Group UK Ltd.
Pitfield, Milton Keynes, MK11 3LW, UK
UKHW041840200726
13854UKWH00003BA/1237

9 781304 345707